2.25

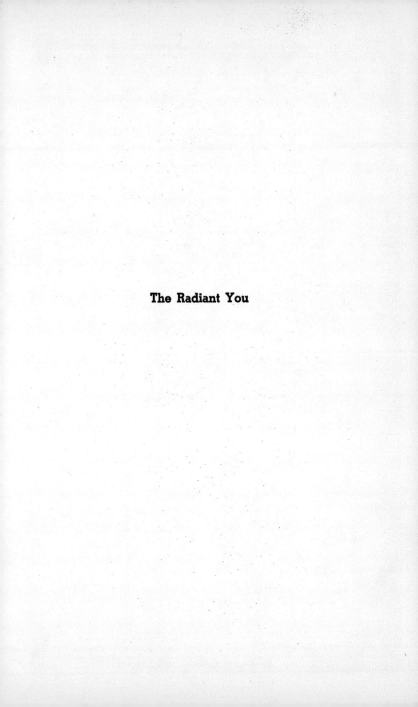

# The Radiant You

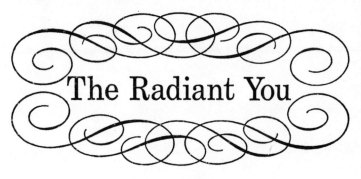

# The Radiant You

Marge Caldwell

BROADMAN PRESS • Nashville, Tennessee

*To Chuck*

*my husband*

*for his confidence in me*

*which along with his genuine*

*love and encouragement*

*made this book possible*

# PREFACE

       In today's world with all of its confusion and tragedy . . . yet its mighty challenge . . . there stands tall and straight our modern youth! America's future has always been in the hands of her youth, but never before have the young people been caught up in the affairs of America's present as now.

I believe a terrible injustice has been done to our modern youth by lumping them together and calling them "teen-agers," as if it were a disease. At a time when life should be budding into one of the most exciting eras in their lives, some adults have branded them in terms of the minority. Let's start thinking in terms of the majority of young people who very quietly make their mark . . . fight their battles heroically . . . conquer their "inner man" . . . live normally clean lives . . . love God and their fellowman.

One student expressed it like this: "We haven't really been challenged or tested by a great war or depression as yet. Our greatest concern is that we may not get the job because of our poor grade average. The pressure's on! That's why the mass scale of cheating in high school and college!" Another said: "I just don't have a sense of mission and adventure . . . the incentive is missing!"

Yet, in the midst of all of this, there is a bright, wonderful hope! I have worked with teen-age girls for several years in my charm and modeling school: I have watched as they've developed in the art of modeling; I have thrilled as I saw them master the mechanics of that art; *but* my greatest joy has been the opportunity and privilege to help them develop inner radiance. The mechanics can be taught—the inner radiance must be caught. It is this radiance that comes from Jesus Christ and makes one not only live—but be *alive!*

Who is the teen-age girl? She is the mother of tomorrow. She will marry someday and become her husband's helper, and be the mother of his children. She it is who will pass on to the next generation the social grace and polish of today's civilization. Her voice, low, clear, and sweet will be heard the length and breadth of the land. It is she who will fight for peace—with love and good will rather than with blood and hate. The girls of today will not be of the beat generation . . . but of an unbeatable one!

> Nobody knows what a girl is worth,
> The world must wait and see,
> But every power behind the throne
> Is a girl that used to be.

Appreciation is due my wonderful family and friends who have encouraged me to write this book. My deep gratitude to Mrs. Jim Henry of Midland, Texas for typing the manuscript.

MARGE CALDWELL

# Contents

# The Radiant You

# 1

## SPIRITUAL SPARKLE

May I come in for just a minute? Whether it's in the quiet of the school library, or the confusion of your room—would you let me intrude?

Who am I? It really doesn't matter. As I passed the door and looked in, I saw a lovely young woman, with a youthful sophistication that didn't quite hide the puzzled and concerned expression mirrored on her face and in her eyes.

Were you thinking, as you perched on that chair, about the questions of *your* life? Did your thoughts run something like this: "Where do I go from here? What is the meaning of life? Where do I fit in in this picture? What's it all about, anyway? Is there a goal for me? Why fight it —why not give in and join the crowd?"

Perhaps you hear a still, small voice that keeps saying, "There's more to life than the humdrum usual routine. There's excitement and challenge, and a great love for me out there, somewhere. God made me, and he made me for *something!*"

It seems like such a shame that it is humanly possible —to go through this life and entirely miss the wonderful, fulfilling, and exciting meaning of it all! Yet God has planted inside each of us a yearning to reach beyond ourselves. Would you like to have that inner something that brings joy, peace, enchantment, and security?

Ah-h-h! *Now.* I have your attention! Who *doesn't* yearn for all of this? Christ tells us in the Bible that it can be ours for the asking. Too simple? Too uncomplicated? Your friend may tell you that it's just too "unreal" and to "get with it and stop dreaming"! Will you spare me just a few more minutes?

I call this wonderful ingredient that makes life become more than existence *Spiritual Sparkle.* So many people substitute "things" in the place of this experience. Sometimes we are so busy *doing* that we miss the beauty of *experiencing* and *being!* In Philippians 4:13, the apostle Paul wrote, "I can do all things through Christ which strengtheneth me." This opens channels of ability we never thought we had—and gives us strength that we never dreamed of. You've heard these Scripture passages quoted before—and you may have learned them in your church; but, somehow, they were just memorized or listened to and *never* became a part of you.

In the past years, my husband and I have counseled with many young people on high school and college campuses. We feel a deep compassion for the students of our day. Take *you* for instance. You are on the campus of a large school, and it's so different and large and lonely —sometimes you are completely confused. The concepts that were a part of your home and training have taken on a different light. You feel a sense of rebellion mingled with a sense of futility creeping over you. Oh, yes, add a sense of guilt, too! Down deep inside of you, where only you and your God actually see, you have a desire to be more than the picture our modern society paints of youth. You want to rise above the sordid and perverted scene into which you have been thrust, and to surpass the mediocre level that seems to be the current goal. Right?

True, there are many young people who are steeped in delinquency. They have been hurt and destroyed by the sordid environment into which they have been born. On the other hand, there is also a great multitude of youth with a deep desire to *be* something, to contribute something of grandeur to this earth, to catch the spark "that falls down from above."

I teach classes in poise and charm, professionally, to the young people and adults of the area in which I live. It is through this channel that many opportunities have been opened to me to speak to our youth. As I teach these young people, I stress to them the importance of realizing that their lives are made up of four facets: physical, mental, emotional, and spiritual. As they learn to be their best selves physically, by learning the mechanics of posture, standing, sitting, and such, we talk constantly of the potential for "good grooming" that *God* gives them —beauty of hair, eyes, complexion, teeth. We emphasize the importance of gratitude in their hearts for the bodies so wonderfully made that are theirs. To be their best, physically, means to make the most of their good points and to minimize those physical traits that seem to bother them so often.

As we think of the mental area of our lives, I challenge you to be your *best*—reminding you that your best may not compare favorably with the best in some people, but it will far surpass the best in others. We are not required nor expected to be more than we are capable of being— however it is so sad to see a young person with great potential who neglects or ignores this power. Did you realize that everything you see, hear, or experience is stored away carefully by your subconscious mind and becomes the well of knowledge over the years which enriches your life, or destroys it? That is why it is so im-

portant to read the works and writings of the truly great
men, and to stop filling your minds with the pornographic
material (that could rightfully be called "trash") and
movies that present sex in the basest of ways. Where is
the movie that challenges the best in you? Where is the
play that brings realism to the screen—yet, gives the
moral integrity of the individual the importance which
it deserves? Oh, yes, some very few are presented to
you! Thank God that there are a few adults left who care
more about encouraging our youth than in money made
by exploiting them!

Now, let's look at your emotional life! Ah-h-h! This
is where you have the greatest joy and also the most
trouble!

If I could just control my emotions, you think. Well,
you may not be able to do this alone, but you and God
can. It is in this area that your life can be enriched beyond your wildest dreams, or you can be utterly undone.
Would you like to feel that someone walks beside you
and guides you? That is not an impossibility. But God
will not force his way into your heart and life—you must
invite him in. Rest assured that if you ask Christ to come
in and take over your life and heart, he will. Being in the
will of God for so many young people means that they
feel they might have to give up something. They think
it will make them some kind of oddball! Have you been
thinking this? Nothing could be farther from the truth.
Christ takes the individual, adds a new ingredient, and
then she begins to live. Yes, you guessed it! He has added
*spiritual sparkle* to her heart, which is reflected in her
life! *Then* she becomes a well-adjusted individual who
reflects his glory no matter where she is. Is she odd? Is
she different? Not odd, but different. She is well on her
way to becoming beautifully poised and charming.

Do you feel a deep sense of need? Is there a lack of

spiritual depth and meaning? Or is there a feeling that God is someone very far away—somebody up there who loves me—maybe. I challenge you to ask him to fill your life full, to give to you that added substance of which spiritual maturity is made. Ask him to come into your heart—and then you will gradually feel your life take on new meaning. Christian poise and charm can be yours, and then God, himself, adds the superlative—*spiritual sparkle!*

# 2

## BETWEEN US GIRLS

None of us can stand to take an honest look at ourselves very often because we just can't stand what we see! Most of the time, we rationalize what we are and do by saying! "Well, I really didn't have anything to do with that because I wasn't the president or chairman. Now, if *I* had been in charge of it, I would have . . ." Or, "If I had had all the advantages *she's* had . . ." Or, "Well, my family's never really understood me, and it's all their fault that I'm the way I am." Or, "Well, God made me like this and I can't help it."

Repulsive? Oh, my, yes! Untrue? Well, certainly! It is true that our backgrounds do color what we are, but we can rise above our backgrounds and situations if we really want to. God is the one who can hold our hand while we do it. So let's ask him to hold our hand now while we look at *you!* Let's see who you *really* are. Are you ready? Have you eaten a large breakfast? Do you feel honest and strong enough to take it? Here goes!

### What Mask Are You Wearing?

Are you wearing a mask? Do you put on a front on Sunday and get a real pious look on your face to enter the church? Do you wear a mask to school? How about your parties? And the family? Do you wear a mask there at home with them? Of course not! Not there! At home you can be your old ugly self and cause confusion and worry, and they have to put up with it, don't they? Why? Well, because they love you, and, anyway, you belong to them. That's what they get for having you. . . is that what you're thinking? Besides, it's *fun* to pay them back for being so "out of it" and old-fashioned.

We all wear masks, and yet, we know that Jesus condemned hypocrisy and role-playing more than anything else in the Bible. Today, if we don't like the role we have to play, we just take a pep pill or tranquilizer and that helps us play the role better. With a tranquilizer, we may not play the role very well, but we just don't care!

We're all guilty of this. I shall never forget what my high-school-senior daughter said to me one Sunday morning. My husband, Chuck (he's fabulous!), and Gay and I were dressing for Sunday School—I was supposed to get there early that morning. I had reminded my family of this about ten times. They were talking and laughing. They weren't hurrying like I thought they should. I was getting madder and madder by the minute. Finally, we left about five minutes late. I hate to tell you this but I was livid. I kept thinking how unnecessary and thoughtless this was, and how they had ignored me. I proceeded to tell them about it all the way to church. The more I talked about it the worse it seemed. By the time we were parking in front of the church, I told them everything in the world I could think of that I hadn't liked for the last two weeks. As we parked, I noticed one of the young girls in my Sunday School class parking beside us. I smiled broadly and said: "Good morning, Jewell. How are *you* this bright and shining morning? Isn't this a beautiful day?"

Gay looked at me carefully, and then said very quietly, "Mother, you can turn it off and turn it on quicker than anyone I've ever seen."

I thought of grounding her for two weeks and calling it grounding for impudence. However, a still, small voice kept telling me that I was guilty of—well, *you* know! So I went on to class, but deep down inside me I asked God to forgive me for wearing that horrible mask. Later, I asked Gay to forgive me for losing control before church and having to wear a mask in front of my student.

### *On Balance?*

One morning, I woke up and started to get out of bed. I had felt just fine when I retired, but now, all of a sudden, I couldn't stand up, or sit up, or *anything!* I didn't know what on earth was the matter, but I found out later that I had something by a long medical name which meant an inner-ear infection. That was the most terrifying thing that had ever happened to me. I had completely lost my balance. It took a few days and shots for me to recover, but I decided that I have never appreciated my inner ear. I decided that balance is very important, and you know what? You simply cannot become completely balanced until you *really* know yourself!

Let me ask you a few questions! Are you an introvert? Quiet? Unassuming? Are you a "loner"? Do you like to spend hours thinking great thoughts, or reading truly fine literature, or listening to beautiful music? Well, then . . . do not fret because you are not vivacious and exciting! Let's see what you're like. So you're quiet. How wonderful! Did you know that Jesus used the quiet people, too? Did you realize that Andrew, the quiet one, was the one who found the secret of Jesus first . . . and then passed it on to his boisterous brother? God made you like you are for a purpose. Now, *your* job is to find that purpose, not to sit and sigh because you aren't like someone else. Isn't it exciting to you that with all the millions of people God has made, there isn't one that is just like another? Not even twins! They are different in personality, even if their physical beings are alike. I've always thought that God must have a terrific sense of humor. Know why? Well, just look around you. Aren't we a funny lot most of the time? And yet God loves us. Now, that's a miracle if I've ever seen one.

You say that this is not the picture of you. You're loud and boisterous and crave attention from the other kids. and will do anything in the world to get it, even if it takes compromising your goals and convictions. You're an extrovert? That's great! You have a lot going for you right at the beginning. But don't ruin it. Laughing too loud, talking about silly things to just fill in the conversational gap, trying to be the life of the party incessantly, these are the things that you catch yourself doing, yet hating yourself for it all the time. No one would even guess how self-conscious you really are, would they? All right, admit it! You're tired of it, and you would like to be a great girl in every sense of the word. You have the personality for it, so there's nothing in the world that can hinder you. Would you like to be your best self? Your best self is just what God wants you to be!

I can hear you saying that you don't fit into either of these categories! You're really an in-between, not a whole lot of anything, and just a little of everything. Do you feel colorless? I received a letter from one young lady who said: "I don't really think very much of myself. I don't get excited about anything, I don't especially like or dislike to do anything—I'm just a big bore who is bored stiff with herself.

She has not found herself yet, for underneath that boredom and dislike of her kind of person is a personality, just screaming to be loved and noticed.

I know you're thinking in your mind while you read this, "All right. So I'm that kind of person! What can I do?

Wait just a minute. We haven't finished searching ourselves yet!

## Do You Believe in Miracles?

Do you really believe in miracles? Or, do you just smile and say, "My experience with God is real, I know, but there's no need to just get carried away by this thing of daily faith in miracles." Please don't close your mind to this. Christ performs miracles daily, now, just as he did ages ago when he walked on the earth. But the condition is that he performs them in our lives to the degree that we have faith that he will. He said, "Be careful (anxious) for nothing; but in every thing by prayer and supplication with thanksgiving let your requests be made known unto God. And the peace of God, which passeth all understanding, shall keep your hearts and minds through Christ Jesus" (Phil. 4:6-7). In the Gospel of Mark, he told us, "Therefore I say unto you, What things soever ye desire, when ye pray, believe that ye receive them, and ye shall have them" (11:24). Remember, he was talking to those who had a genuine experience with him and who had accepted him as Saviour! That is the first condition. Then, with faith, we can ask him to come into our lives and change them with his own radiance.

Many years ago, in the door of the Temple at Jerusalem at the gate called Beautiful, sat a man who was crippled. Now, he wasn't just handicapped a little, but he had been badly crippled from birth and had never walked.

His friends and family took him every day and laid him
at this gate and he begged for everything he had. Can
you imagine what this man thought? Can you believe
anyone would want to live like this? This man wasn't living, he was existing! What a horrible existence! Then
one day he was carried down to the gate. This seemed
a day like every other dull day he'd lived. Little did he
know that this was to be a banner day in his life—that his
whole life would be changed today. And that's the exciting thing about us. One day may seem like every
other dull day, and, then, Jesus comes to us in the form
of a friend, a call, an opportunity we'd never dreamed
of, and our lives are changed overnight.

Two men were walking toward the lame man and the
Bible tells us that they were Peter and John. I can just
see him looking at them and wondering if they were going to give him any money. Wonder of all wonders! They
were stopping! How they were staring at him! And then
Peter was speaking: "Silver and gold have I none; but
such as I have give I thee: In the name of Jesus Christ
of Nazareth rise up and walk" (Acts 3:6).

Do you think that lame man said, "No sir, you see I've
never walked a day in my life. My legs are shriveled
and knotted and I'd be too weak to walk." No! The
Bible says that Peter took him by the right hand and
lifted him up, and immediately his feet and ankle bones
received strength. Then he began leaping for joy! There's
not a word there about his hesitating and making ex-
cuses for his lameness, refusing to believe that Jesus
could heal him. Do you know what happened then? All
the people began running from everywhere to see what
on earth had happened to the lame man. They could
hardly believe their eyes. How he'd changed! In that
very moment, that man began to live and quit just existing.

### The Answer!

Would you like to have an answer to yourself? Of course you would, we all would, and we all want to know ourselves! So here goes!

1. Ask Christ to come into your heart and life and become your Saviour. There's no other place to start than right there! He is the author of *Spiritual Sparkle,* and, after all, he made you so he should know you better than anyone else. When I'm physically ill, I want to go to *my* doctor, to someone that I *know* knows me and is interested in *me*. When we are in need of spiritual help, who would be better than the One who made us and knows exactly what our need is before we tell him? Tell him how you feel. You don't need to be a theological giant to talk to him—ask him right where you are!

2. Now you are in a position to talk to him as his child. Remember that he is anxious to give you good things, and to make your life victorious. Jesus said, "I am come that they might have life, and that they might have it more abundantly" (John 10:10). Why don't we just stop right here and thank him for all he's done for us and tell him we love him? I know that sometimes Chuck will just out of a clear blue sky say, "Marge, I love you so much!" I get weak and goose bumpy. It's a thrill to be told that out of a clear blue sky—or out of any kind of sky for that matter! How much our Heavenly Father must be pleased when we express our love for him.

3. Accept yourself as you *are!* Quit fuming because you aren't personable like Mary, or talkative like Judy, or beautiful like Doris. There's just one you so be the *best* you God ever made. If you're a leader, then be one. But don't look down your nose at those who can't lead— this is misusing your talent. If you think you'll *die* if you have to say one word out loud, then don't force yourself to do that! Be the kind of quiet person that you are, but when you say something, make it worth listening to.

4. Respect yourself. If you have no self-respect, you can't expect others to respect you. Love yourself! Oh, I don't mean that kind of person with "I" trouble. You know, "I, I, I," all the time. Jesus said for us to love our neighbors as we love ourselves. We have to live with ourselves all the time, and, if we begin to hate ourselves and belittle ourselves constantly, we will lose our self-respect. Humility is not in degrading yourself, it is in forgetting yourself.

5. Quit talking, as a Christian, about what you don't do, and begin *being* something! On many campuses I've heard young people say, "I don't do this, and I don't do that," and I just want to say, "Well, bully for you! Now tell me what you *do!*"

It's a trite saying, I know—"What you are speaks so loud, I can't hear a word you say"—but it is so true! If you become the kind of person who stands for something, instead of one who stands for nothing, then you've found the secret of the radiant life.

How about it? Do you think it's worth trying? Are you tired of just existing? Is yours just a humdrum, daily routine, full of boredom and self-torture? Then let's do something about it! Remember, you can't do it alone, but with God, all things are possible!

# 3

## IS YOUR SLIP SHOWING?

Oh, I'm not really talking about your slip! I mean, are you really well-groomed, or have you just barely missed the mark of good grooming? Some girls have the know-how of being well-groomed; but, when they make their entrance, I keep thinking they've left off something, or added just a little too much! Self-confidence is knowing you are doing and wearing the right thing in any given situation. Someone has said that self-confidence is the feeling you have just before you know better! But that's a joke, because when you know how to meet a situation and you feel correctly dressed, you just naturally feel more self-confident.

One day, in one of my Saturday classes of fifteen-year-old girls, I had been talking about poise. I had told the class that poise was self-control under trying circumstances. A person who is beautifully poised apparently has control of the situation. Early that morning, Chuck had asked me to mail a very important letter for him at noon, and he wanted me to mail it downtown in the post office. Since I was going to a very "dressed-up" luncheon at noon, I just dressed for the occasion before my class. When the class was over, I went to my bedroom and put on my white gloves and my *very* frivolous, feathered hat. I took a long look in the mirror, and hesitated. *You* know how we do, girls, when we think no one is looking! I thought to myself, "Old girl, you're not so bad!"

I got into my car, drove downtown, and parked across the street from the post office. It was noon and very crowded! I stood on the corner waiting for the light to change to green. It changed and I stepped down off the curb. Somehow my ankle turned, and, in a flash, I was sprawled out in the middle of the street.

Now I want to back up and tell you that in my town there is a very austere and sophisticated man, with a deep voice, who makes me feel like I have two heads, or a run in my hose, or chipped fingernail polish. Do you know anyone like this? I am invariably seated by him at dinner parties and come into contact with him in many places. He doesn't talk loudly but makes a deep, guttural sound in his words as he drawls them out. Now, if there was anyone in the world that I didn't want to see right then, and especially in that position, it was he. But there he was, standing right behind me, drawling: "Mrs. Caldwell, are you hurt?"

"Oh, no! Of course not!" I replied.

I did hope that I was bleeding, because then it might have been worth it! As I landed on my all fours, I had hurled my purse into the middle of the street. It flew open, and all the lipsticks, notes, pencils, pens, gum, wallet, pictures, and such, flew in every direction. I have a bad habit of writing things on little slips of paper as I think of them during the day (at my age you *have* to . . . they may never come by this way again!), and there they were all over the street. As I fell, my beautiful, flowered hat jarred over onto my face and eyes. I nearly died! I thought for a moment that I had gone blind. My white gloves were ruined, for I had "slud" (there is no other word to describe it!) on them on the dirty pavement!

"Would you please get my purse and things?" I asked my sophisticated friend.

There he was, the perfect picture of the modern-day man of distinction, on his knees in the middle of the street. People are so ugly when they get in cars! Perfectly lovely people turn into demons behind steering wheels! They would do a double take and stare at both of us, and then just laugh themselves to death! What could I do? I had runs in both hose, my hat pushed to the back of my head so that I could see, and filthy gloves. I just scooted back and sat down on the curb (but I kept my knees together like a lady should!), and my friend sat down beside me. We began talking and laughing, and then you should have seen them stare! The modeling teacher and Mr. Sophistication himself, sitting on the curb downtown at noon, laughing as if that were the normal thing to do!

I feel very close to my friend now, and we love sitting next to each other at parties. Our conversation invariably starts with, "Do you remember that day . . .? or someone will say, "Marge, tell us how to have poise . . . especially on your all fours at noon downtown!"

### Posture Pills

Have you had your posture pill this morning? What on earth do I mean? Oh, I mean "How do you stack up?" You don't like pills so early in the day? Well, if you take *this* pill early, you'll see a definite change! Posture is the backbone of confidence and charm. Do you look like you could whip your weight in wildcats? Or, do you look like you will fall down if the wind blows on you? Does your posture betray self-consciousness and carelessness, or does it say to the world that you intend to conquer life?

Oh, c'mon! Let's take the posture pill. Who knows? It may make an exciting change even today. Now! Tuck in your hips . . . pull your chest up . . . tighten your abdomen (stomach, that is!) muscles . . . hold shoulders relaxed . . . hang arms loosely . . . lift your weight out of your waistline . . . make long distance between your chest and abdomen . . . straighten your spine . . . ALL THE WAY UP NOW! . . . AND LIFT YOUR RIB CAGE (*you* know, where your ribs are!). Don't be settled . . . nor strained . . . nor still . . . ONLY ONE "S" . . . STRETCHED!!!

Now! *That* wasn't so bad, was it? Try it every morning, hold the position till you count five . . . slowly (now don't cheat!) and see what happens! Remember, some clothes look better on hangers because the hangers are straight. The most expensive, most beautifully designed dresses lose their style on a girl who droops. A girl with good posture can wear simple, inexpensive clothes and be attractive. Do try the posture pill!

### Grooming Granules

I thought it might be helpful if I gave you a list of wonderful hints to grooming. See how many of these you already know or do—just see how you "stack up" here:

1. What about my makeup during sleep? *Never, no never,* go to bed with your makeup on! Let your skin breathe and sleep well, too!

2. What can I do about "clammy" hands? Just use an antiperspirant on the palms of your hands. Amazing how that will solve your problem.

3. What should I weigh? When you are going by a weight chart, take into consideration whether you are small- or large-boned.

4. What about perfume? By all means, use it—or better, use a good spray cologne. Spray it around your hair, as well as on you. If you're the "outdoorsy" type, don't choose a mysterious scent. If you're the dainty, fragile type, don't select a heavy cologne. In fact, a fresh, clean, light perfume is very good for summer for everyone. Remember, don't drown your date in the odor—just a pleasant aroma will do.

5. Is deodorant a necessity? Probably nothing in your grooming is more important than a good deodorant. Never leave it off.

6. If I wear sleeveless dresses? Never forget that cleanliness and care show here more than anywhere. Remember the razor and deodorant. And this goes for legs, too—the razor, I mean! You don't want to look like you have "porcupine" legs.

7. What if I'm too tall? *Never, never* slump! Stand tall and be proud of it. Be poised and queenly, remembering that the best models are tall and stately.

8. My hair is a mess! There are color rinses and frosting—all kinds of helps now for our hair. But most important: brush, brush, brush! Take care of your hair—it can be your best asset. Shampoo as often as it needs it.

9. What can I do about my complexion? Keep it clean! Use a mild soap and water, or a good cleanser—whatever your particular skin can take. Take a tablespoon of lemon juice first thing every morning in a little water. In a few weeks, your skin will begin to look better! Remember, regularity in this not only helps your complexion but also will aid any problem of elimination.

10. What can I do about my teeth? Brush well after meals whenever possible . . . plus well-balanced meals . . . plus lots of vitamin C. Remember, it's those teeth that will make or break a smile!

11. What if the current "in" color or fashion is not good for me? Then, by all means, do *not* conform to it completely! If the color for fall happens to be Temple Gold, and you look like you have yellow jaundice in

Temple Gold—don't wear it! Choose a scarf or pin in that color and let it go at that, or if you look like a string bean in a shift, wear a slightly pleated skirt and a "Poor Boy" that fits loosely. If you make a bikini look like it's going around without a body, choose a one-piece swimsuit. If you are on the chubby side, choose a loose-fitting garment.

12. How do I know for *sure* if I'm correctly dressed . . . not overdressed or underdressed? Here is a good rule to go by. It is called the "Rule of 14." You count your clothing and accessories, and, if you have on more than fourteen points, you're overdressed. If you have on less than seven points, you're underdressed. It will really work! Look at the chart on page 32. Just check yourself every time you dress. Pretty soon, you can count yourself before I can say "cool"!

*Now!* Count yourself the next time you dress for a date and see how you come out. If you will stick to this rule, you will never be in doubt. Young people tend to underdress and adults tend to overdress. Help your mother, too. It can be fun!

13. Does it matter if my shoes are a *tiny* bit scuffed? Yes, it does! You can have on a perfectly beautiful outfit and have on shoes that look like "they've had it" and it ruins your "well-groomed" look. Now, I know that loafers that look new make you sick, but keep your shoes *clean* and the heels "well-heeled."


REMEMBER! THE MOST IMPORTANT THING THAT YOU WILL WEAR IS YOUR SMILE, SO SMILE . . . SMILE . . . SMILE!!!

## *What the Boys Say!*

Not long ago I decided to take a poll of some young men on high-school and college campuses to test their feelings about girls in many different areas. We hear so much about how boys feel about various things, so

## RULE OF 14

| | | | | |
|---|---|---|---|---|
| Dress | Multicolored | 2 pts. | Solid color | 1 pt. |
| Shoes | Trimmed, multicol. | 2 pts. | Solid color | 1 pt. |
| Purse | Trimmed, multicol. | 2 pts. | Solid color | 1 pt. |
| Gloves | Trimmed, multicol. | 2 pts. | Solid color | 1 pt. |
| Hose | Textured or lace | 2 pts. | Regular hose | 1 pt. |
| Scarf | Multicolored | 2 pts. | Solid color | 1 pt. |
| Hairtrim | Multicolored | 2 pts. | Solid color | 1 pt. |
| Sweater | Multicolored | 2 pts. | Solid color | 1 pt. |
| Coat | Fur-trimmed, plaid | 2 pts. | Solid color | 1 pt. |
| Hat | Trimmed, multicol. | 2 pts. | Untrimmed | 1 pt. |
| Wristwatch | Jeweled | 2 pts. | Plain | 1 pt. |
| Glasses | Jeweled | 2 pts. | Plain | 1 pt. |
| Bracelet | Ornate | 2 pts. | Plain | 1 pt. |
| Rings | Jeweled | 2 pts. | Plain | 1 pt. |
| Necklace | More than one strand | 2 pts. | One strand | 1 pt. |
| (Chain . . . 1 pt. and drop. . . . 1 pt | | | | |
| Earrings | Jeweled | 2 pts. | Plain | 1 pt. |
| Pin | Jeweled | 2 pts. | Plain | 1 pt. |
| Ankle Bracelet | | 1 pt. | | |

I decided to go straight to the horse's mouth. Now these horses . . . uh, I mean, boys, said some very interesting things. Some of them you will like and some of them you won't! But I present them to you, and I think it will be a good idea for you to think carefully about them.

Do you know why?

Because I tried to choose young men who would represent a cross section of our youth and also our college campuses.

One boy is a star "footballer," playing center and linebacker. He's listed in *Who's Who in the Industrial Arts* field and has had several awards in various other fields. He is very popular with the student body, "knows what's going on," and is a fine Christian. Another one was voted "Most Congenial" in his senior class. He loves everybody and everybody loves him. He grins all the time, and has blonde hair, blue eyes, and dimples. (Now quit drooling!) He is a man's man in every sense of the word, but thinks girls are definitely here to stay! Another young man is head cheerleader, and has gotten so many awards that there's not room enough here to list them all. He was voted the "Most Friendly" in his senior class, and is tall and go-o-od looking. One whom I interviewed is president of both the student body, and the Student Council, and has been class favorite each year of high school. He is a member of the National Honor Society and has lettered in baseball and basketball. The rest of them are leaders in their fields. On their campuses, they are considered real cool.

These are the ideas they gave me as I interviewed them individually.

*Hair*—"I like long hair . . . shoulder-length hair is *great* . . . casual hairdos send me . . . teasing or backcombing is okay if not too much . . . I like hair bows."

*Makeup*—"I like it if I can't see too much of it . . . like the natural look . . . hate white lipstick . . . love pale colors in lipstick . . . not too much eye makeup, sometimes they look like they've been sick a year!"

*Appearance*—"I always notice dress first . . . I want her to be neat and smell good . . . like casual dress better . . . doesn't necessarily have to be cute and pretty, just neat and clean . . . like girl who takes pride in her appearance . . . I feel good when she fixes up pretty for me . . . don't like overweight girls . . . can't stand long fingernails, I feel like she's got claws . . . I think miniskirts are on their way out and I'm glad, 'cause I don't like knobby knees . . . want her to look feminine . . . like dresses that leave something to the imagination . . . like pierced ears and wild earrings . . . hate rollers in hair in public . . . can't *stand* to see a girl with a toothpick in her mouth!"

*Personality*—"I can't stand insincerity . . . like a good mixer who isn't always the center of attention . . . comfortable with good conversationalist . . . I like a girl who is the same to everyone, regardless of who they are . . . like a girl with high morals . . . like to date someone who laughs a lot . . . she ought to have a strong relationship with God . . . don't like a conceited girl . . . don't like someone who makes fun of others . . . can't stand fake actions . . . don't like for her to talk to other girls about me."

*Dating*—"I like to date a genuine girl . . . like one who respects herself . . . I want her to have family pride . . . can't stand ill-mannered girls . . . don't want her to giggle all the time . . . don't like flirting with others when with me . . . don't like for them to talk about me to others . . . I lose interest when they drive by my house and honk all the time . . . I don't want to be chased . . . I want her to sit close to me (little past the middle) in the car, but not on me . . . don't want her to call me on the phone . . . unless she has a reason . . . I avoid girls who chase . . . going steady is great because you always have a date . . . I think young people get in trouble easier when they go steady . . . don't want my date to smoke . . . I think smoking looks cheap and smells bad, too, if *you* don't smoke . . . besides it bothers my sinus . . . I lose interest in a girl who will let me go as far as I want to with her . . . I want a kiss to mean something, not to pay me for a date . . . I'm hesitant not to park because I think maybe she wants to . . . would like to go in her house every now and then and watch the late, late movie and eat . . . I like for her to keep up with what's going on . . . don't want a girl to be obvious about a goodnight kiss . . . I want a girl to call a halt in making out, because I'll go as far as she'll let me . . . I *hate* for girls to lead me on . . . nothing's as repulsive as a drunk girl . . . I prefer one who doesn't drink, I feel proud of her . . . beer can mess a girl up quicker than I can . . . drinking takes away from her charm."

## *Is Change Possible?*

I want to tell you a story. The wonderful thing about this story is that it is completely true. I know a girl can change because I was on hand and watched it happen to a young friend of mine. I'll call her Judy.

I had gone to Arizona as a modeling and charm teacher. My daughter and I were to be at this camp for six weeks, and it was one of the most wonderful and rewarding six weeks I have ever spent. When camp got started and I met with my first modeling class that day (my course was compulsory), I had so many cute girls I could hardly stand it. Among them was Judy. She

glared at me and slumped around, and was dressed in
*very* tight blue jeans and an old shirt. She couldn't,
have cared less about modeling, and didn't like anything
but horses and swimming. However, she was forced to
take this class. She was about twenty pounds overweight,
had bushy eyebrows like Groucho Marx, hair in a stiff
ponytail, and was the picture of rebellion.

I said to her, "Judy, stand up straight and let me see
how you look."

"I'm standing as straight as I can, and I don't want
to take this course anyway!"

I thought to myself, If I can get this girl to change,
I'll deserve a medal.

Every day the other girls would tell me how Judy
argued about religion with everyone with whom she
came in contact. Each night we had vespers, and immediately she would get into an argument with the
girls about Christianity, God, or anything that dealt with
religion. She claimed to be an agnostic, said there really
wasn't a God, and laughed at the faith of the others.
She succeeded in thoroughly confusing a large group of
girls.

One lovely evening after vespers, she approached
me. "Mrs. Caldwell," she said, "I want to talk to you
about religion."

I answered, "No, Judy, I don't argue about religion.
I know God is not dead, I love Christ with all my heart,
and I do not argue about it."

"I don't want to argue," she continued, "but there are
some things that I'd like to know."

I thought to myself, "now, I'll just see if she's serious.
I'll make it hard for her.

"We'll, Judy," I stalled, "you know I'm a counselor
in a cabin and do not have a lot of extra time. If you
really want to talk about it, I'll be glad to. We'll have

to meet at 5:30 tomorrow morning on the porch of my cabin. Will you be there?"

"That's a deal," she called back over her shoulder as she ran over to the canteen.

What in the world had I done? Five-thirty in the morning? I'd lost my mind! I'm not alert at 8:00 A.M., much less 5:30! However, I set my alarm, and before I could get dressed the next morning, she was there. We went out into that indescribably beautiful Arizona morning—crisp, cool, and quiet—and sat down under a small mesquite tree. We began talking, and all of her questions and rebellions rolled out! Finally, about an hour and a half later, I opened my Bible and showed Judy how to become a Christian. She accepted Christ right there. Her prayer asking him to come into her heart and life was one of the most halting, yet precious, prayers I've ever heard in all of my life. I then thanked him for coming into her life. As we prepared to leave, I put out my hand and said, "Happy Birthday, Judy! This is your birthday. You've been born again today." Large tears rolled down her cheeks as she asked if she might go tell the camp director, Mrs. Kennerly, what had happened to her that morning. How thrilled we all were at the change that *immediately* began to take place in Judy's life. First, she apologized to most of the girls for her rude and discourteous attitudes toward them.

Soon, she came to me and asked for a Bible. We got a Bible for her and marked some Scripture passages that would be especially helpful to her right then.

One day in modeling class, she said, "Mrs. Caldwell, I really want to learn how to model. And don't you think something should be done about my eyebrows and hair?"

I was thrilled to death, and immediately we put her on a diet. We practically *sat* on her and plucked her eyebrows, cut her hair in a fashionable style, and taught her about the styles that would be most flattering to her figure.

As weeks passed, Judy became the subject of conversation in camp. She learned to model quickly because she wanted to learn! She quit slumping and walked with a lilt that was noticeable to everyone. She began to memorize Scripture passages and came back often for me to mark some more for her. She laughed a lot, teased a lot, and, in a very short time, won the girls over as friends. I have never seen a girl so happy. She had changed before our very eyes. But, girls, what I want you to remember is that the real change came on the inside first, and then we began to see results on the outside.

The last day of camp and we were all going to board the train for home. I was to be on the same train as Judy and, as we traveled back to Texas, we became sad and homesick for the wonderful days we'd experienced back in Arizona.

Judy asked, "Mrs. Caldwell, will you get off the train when we get to my home and meet my family?"

"Of *course!*" I replied. "What time do we get there?"

"Three-thirty in the morning," she said.

Three-thirty! In the morning! Oh, me! But, of course, I wanted to meet her family and was anxious to see them when they saw the new Judy.

When we stepped off the train, there they were. Her mother, father, and brother looked eagerly for her. She hugged them all and then turned and introduced them to me. We talked a few minutes and then Judy asked, "Mother, do you see anything different about me?"

"Why, yes! Your hair is cut . . . and your eyebrows . . . where are they? Oh, you've lost weight, and you look wonderful!"

"But don't you notice something else?" she asked.

"Wel-l-l . . . yes, there's something, but I can't put my finger on it," her mother replied. "Your eyes seem different, Judy. Yes, there's something!"

"Mother," Judy returned, "you sent me off to camp to get 'finished,' and I've just gotten started! I'm a Christian now, and I'm happier than I've ever been in my life. Oh, Mother! It's wonderful!"

I told them good-bye and tearfully hugged Judy. As I lay in my berth that night and we sped through Texas, I thanked God for the inner radiance that he had given to a young girl at camp. Before my very eyes I had seen a physical change come over her as a result of the thrilling change that had taken place in her heart.

Is change possible? Oh, yes! But the change that comes only on the outside is temporary because we do it all ourselves. It is always *taught*. However, the change that takes place on the inside is from God and it can only be *caught*. When Christ touches our lives with a spark from above change is inevitable!

# 4

## WHAT'S "NEW" IN MORALITY?

Every now and then, we feel like we're neglected and that no one really loves us. Haven't you felt like this sometimes? The popular way to express it is "feeling sorry for ourselves". We're always embarrassed to admit it, and won't, unless our family or friends catch us and face us with it. I used to wonder how my mother could possibly be so perceptive, until I got to be a mother. Now I know it wasn't that she was that smart . . . I was just so obvious!

Of course, this involves our emotions. You know, our emotions are the feelings that cause us to get into trouble all the time. Did you ever wake up one morning and think, "I'm going to be sweet all day. I'm not going to slam a door, tease my brother, talk smart to my family, or criticize Mary to Jim—I'm going to really be good!"

### Could This Be You?

You get out of the bed and slink to the bathroom, half asleep. You reach for the toothpaste and your little brother has squeezed the tube in half—toothpaste oozes out everywhere! You reach for the eyeliner, and, sure enough, he has been there, too. Your eyeliner is in the box with the airplane glue, because he just *had* to have a black racing car and had run out of paint! Your emotions tell you to go in there in the kitchen and shake him to pieces. Your mind says to keep control. And you do! You start to put your shoes on, and Mimi, your poodle, has become hungry during the night and completely chewed up one of your loafers. It looks like an overripe banana. While you're trying to think how to tell your mother about your shoe, she calls you to breakfast. You sit down, nervous and upset. Your brother reaches in front of you for the toast and turns your glass of milk over, accidentally of course, right into your very own lap. You don't have to say anything because your mother says it all to your brother as she goes into orbit. That's the second glass of spilled milk this morning. Your dad pulls your mother down out of orbit, and breakfast continues.

Now it's car pool time. As you ride to school, your best friend tells you something "for your own good" which just tears you to pieces. Your emotions tell you to spit back some ugly words and hurt her, too, but your mind keeps control. You're doing fine!

You find that you have made a C on the English test, and you needed a B to get your average up. You go to lunch and, across the cafeteria, you see Mary sitting by Jim, *your* Jim, looking like a dying calf. Now Mary is supposed to be your good friend, yet everybody tells you that she's vowed that she'll get him if it's the last thing she does. If she gets him, it'll *be* the last thing she does! The thing that is infuriating is that Jim looks like he's enjoying the scene. Your emotions tell you to go over there and shake Mary, but you know the principal would take a dim view of violence in the cafeteria. Your mind is in control still, so you just sit there and swallow your food whole, and seethe . . . and seethe.

You go home that afternoon and Mother meets you at
the door with that old chewed-up loafer. She hasn't
gotten a chance to say a word, but you burst out crying
hysterically and run to your room and shut the door.
She quietly opens the door and asks what's the matter.
You just sob, and, when she tells you that the loafer
isn't that important, you almost laugh out loud. What
loafer? It's Jim—and your "good friends"—and all of the
other things that have hit you all day. So you just ex-
plode! What's wrong? Why, you're beginning to feel
sorry for yourself. It's those emotions that get involved,
and all the great resolutions in the world can't stand up
before them. You see, this area is so important because
it colors much of our thinking.

## Compared to What?

I have always been so emotional—down in the dumps
one minute for no apparent reason, and on an emotional
mountaintop the next. I used to wonder if this were
normal, but I was afraid to ask anyone because, if it
weren't, they'd probably put me away somewhere! For
years I'd wondered if I were normal and surely hoped
I was. Not very many years ago I went to Glorieta to
a retreat to learn how to lead in the women's work in my
church. Chuck told me to work hard, learn a lot, and
hurry home. I was trying to learn everything I could, and
one evening we were told about morning watch the next
morning. Now, if there's anything that's hard for me, it's
to concentrate early in the morning! But I went. The
pastor who spoke was also a psychologist. All of a sudden I caught his words.

"Have you ever wondered if you were emotionally
normal?" he asked.

I perked up. After so many years of wondering about myself, maybe I was going to find the answer!

He continued, "If you're always down in the dumps, if you're depressed all the time, or if you're always unhappy, you're organically sick. Go see the doctor. And, if you're always on the mountaintop, flitting from peak to peak, you're also sick. Go see the psychiatrist. If you're up and down, up and down, emotionally, you're normal."

I wanted to stand up in that crowd of women and scream, "Look at me! I'm normal!"

When I returned home from the retreat, I was as excited as can be. I had a wonderful surprise for Chuck. As if he didn't already have a pretty good impression of me after all of these years.

He asked, "Was it great? What did you learn? Did you like it?"

I just smiled slowly and said, "Now, Chuck, sit down and let me tell you something wonderful. Yes, I learned a lot and I'm so glad I went. But listen, Honey. Look at me. I'm normal!"

He just looked blank and asked, "Compared to what?"

*I* was the one that looked blank then!

As long as we don't run through the streets screaming or tearing out our hair, we are considered normal. As long as we stay within the limits of what a civilized society says is normal, we are considered to be just that. But you and I know that some of us are much more "normal" than others. Some of us can control our emotions a lot better than others.

## Dates and Emotion!

Let me be very frank with you. It is in the area of your date life that you are most likely to meet trouble as far as your emotions are concerned. You already know

that, don't you? If you're thinking, "What date life!—just
remember this when you begin dating. I'll tell you what,
let's just pretend you're standing in front of your mirror
now, dressing for a very special fella—Jim. Do your
thoughts run something like this:

*Now, tonight when we leave the show, I know he'll
want to go get hamburgers and Cokes—that is, if he has
any money to get them. Then, after that, he'll start driv-
ing around and I know we'll start out toward that place
where the kids park. I know that I shouldn't go, because I really am beginning to like him a lot and I don't
feel very strong when I'm with him. I know what I'll do,
I'll ask him to bring me home, and we'll come in and
look at the late, late movie!*

It's very easy to think straight when it's broad day-
light and you're dressing for your date. It isn't hard at
all to have all kinds of willpower then. But it's mighty
different when you're with him; you've seen a great
show, eaten a hamburger, and now you're heading for
. . . you know where!

A still, small voice says, "Oh, c'mon! Nobody'll know.
Why not? Everybody else does it. Why shouldn't I?"

Another voice that can barely be heard is saying,
"You know what you said in your room tonight. You
know you should suggest that you all go home."

The civil war that takes place inside you would put
America's Civil War to shame! One voice says, "What
if he won't ask me for another date? I'll bet Mary would
go parking with him." Another voice says, "Do you
really want him if you have to get him like that?"

You know how sick it'll make you feel if you lose your
self-respect. Then you pray quietly to God to give you
strength to say and do what you know you must say and
do.

At the door, Jim looks at you in a very special way,

takes your hand, kisses you gently, and whispers, "I love you because you stand for something. Don't ever change." You walk into the house and you haven't touched the floor yet. God did come to your rescue, and somehow you feel closer to Jim than you ever have!

However, you *may* be thinking, That all *sounds* very great, but it doesn't always work out that way. Lots of times you'll lose the guy.

You're right! But let me assure you of one thing. Any young man who says to you, "If you love me, you will," is really saying, "I love *me* so much I don't care what happens to *you!*"

One student on a college campus said to me one night, "Mrs. Caldwell, any girl who falls for that line, 'If you love me, you will,' has just *got* to be out of it."

Usually when I go to the high-school or college campus, I speak in assembly first, and then have conferences and seminars with the students for several days. I have never met one young man deeply in love who has said to me that it didn't make any difference to him what his girl had done sexually before. One student put it this way: "I'd hate to wonder if every guy I met on the campus might know more about my girl than I do."

## Is There a Solution?

This is not the day of the "new morality"! As Billy Graham has said, "This is not a new morality. It is nothing more than the old immorality."

God has said that sexual immorality is sin, and no matter how you and I rationalize and justify our actions, they must stand up before him! Although we live in a time when you are told to "do anything that comes naturally," and that "sexual freedom is the thing," you are still *you* and must live with yourself for the rest of your life. I wish you could go with me to the campuses and listen to the brokenhearted stories of immorality, the sordid result of a trip with LSD, the utter despair of girls who are pregnant, the drunkenness that brings trouble and self-hate the next day. Then the romance of sexual freedom and license turns pale beside it. One young student cried out, "O Mrs. Caldwell, go to them in junior high! Senior high school is too late!"

Well, you might be asking, what is the answer for me? The answer for you is strength to stand up and *be* somebody! *Any* girl can curse and use profane language. That doesn't take any strength and courage at all. *Any* girl can drink or get drunk and desecrate her body. That doesn't take any effort to do. It's easy! *Any* girl can pass her body around to any boy that happens to be there for the moment. *That* doesn't take anything special. It takes courage and faith to care what you are and what you become. This courage and faith come straight from God. I dare you to ask him for it and then to *expect* him to be your strength as he promised he would!

I know the pressures of today are terrific. I talk with girls enough to know what a strain you're under in times like these. But I also know that God is sufficient, and will never let you down if you seek his help! Then one day, one *wonderful* day, you will be standing at the altar with that special young man, and out of your heart will well deep gratitude to the Heavenly Father for giving you the strength and courage to save yourself for your husband. And it's worth it! No matter what the pseudointellectuals of today are telling you, it is definitely worth it.

Have faith that you can believe God's promise to you personally, and he will answer your request.

Let me give you a wonderful verse, 1 Corinthians 10:13, to use in time of temptation. Here it is: "There hath no temptation taken you but such as is common to man: but God is faithful, who will not suffer you to be tempted above that ye are able; but will with the temptation also make a way to escape, that ye may be able to bear it.

# 5

## WE'RE BEHIND YOU!

"We're behind you." I guess I've had these words said to me in my life a hundred times! When I was a teen-ager and someone said them to me, I often wondered if he really meant it, or if he was just trying to make me feel good. Sometimes you may think the adults you know just don't know what's going on, so how in the world could they be behind you?

Not too long ago, a young girl who is a senior in high school called me. I don't think I've ever heard a more desperate voice in all of my life.

"Mrs. Caldwell," she sobbed, "may I please come see you after school today. I'm in a terrible mess!"

"Oh, yes," I replied, and we made the necessary arrangements to talk together. She was to come to my house directly after school. I did not recognize her name when she called and wondered if I had ever seen her before. She said that a friend had told her to call me.

At the appointed time, she came up and knocked on my door. After introductions, we sat down and got acquainted. What a beautiful girl! She had a lovely blonde flip hair style, and the largest blue eyes I had ever seen. She could have done well in any beauty contest. But those eyes! How cold and steely they were! As she talked, she would toss her head this way and that, giving the impression that she "couldn't care less". She poured out one of the most sordid stories of immorality and drinking binges that I have ever heard. I'm not easily shocked at the things I hear, but I found myself profoundly sad as I listened to this girl to whom God had given so much, and saw her throwing her life away so desperately.

At one point, I said, "But, my dear, God loves you! And he cares what you do with your life."

She turned and looked at me. "God and I are not on speaking terms. He doesn't love me."

We talked almost two hours, and I had the feeling that I had completely failed in reaching this girl in any way. She had disclosed a very confused and uncertain background. She kept saying, "I have nobody. My family doesn't care. There's no one to turn to. Do you know how it feels, Mrs. Caldwell, to have absolutely *no* one behind you?"

NO ONE BEHIND YOU! This is utter loneliness! You can be in a room full of people, and feel so terribly alone. Yes! There have been times in my life when I had experienced this same thing. It is indescribably lonely. All this time there had been someone behind me, praying for me, but I didn't know it. It just seemed at the time that I was utterly alone.

I shall never forget one day—one rainy day, when, after school I was just sitting in my room. Everything had gone wrong that day for this sixteen-year-old teen-ager, and my family seemed miles away in their understanding of my situation. I sat there, yes, feeling sorry for myself, and thinking of all the ways I could get even. This was one of the times I particularly remember thinking to myself, Marge, there's just absolutely no one who really understands what you're going through. There's *no* one behind you, understanding and encouraging. And I felt *absolutely* alone!

I was so deep in my own thoughts that I didn't even hear the door to my room quietly open. Someone behind me whispered, "May I intrude a moment?"

I nearly jumped out of my skin! I did recognize the voice, however. This was my mother's best friend, an adult that I had come to love and trust. She just seemed to know about young people, and, as I looked up into her face, I saw just love and understanding, not curiosity and intrusion.

So I opened my mouth and let all the resentment and rebellion pour out. Here was someone who understood! I could trust her and was sure she wouldn't betray my confidence or think less of me as I bared my heart and soul to her. When I had finished, I just laid my head down on the bed and began to cry. She didn't tell me not to. She just sat quietly by and waited. When I looked up with a tear-stained face and swollen eyes (I never could cry daintily . . . I always look sick for hours afterwards), she put her arms around my shoulders, and I'll never forget what she said:

"I know, Marge, that many times you feel that there's absolutely no one who understands your problems. We adults find ourselves in this same dilemma many, many times. I know you feel a desperate need to talk to someone, to share with someone who has had experience in whatever area you're concerned with, and this should probably mean an adult. But where will you find an adult like that? We're all around you, Marge! People who love and appreciate young people and want to help.

"But never forget: the One who really knows and understands is God. Turn to him, for he will always be near and available. He left a special word just for you when you feel like you do today. It is found in Proverbs 3:5-6: 'Trust in the Lord with all thine heart; and lean not unto thine own understanding. In all thy ways acknowledge him, and he shall direct thy paths.' There's nothing as wonderful as the erasing of a feeling of guilt and rebellion from your heart, Marge! God gave you a spiritual eraser, too. It's found in 1 John 1:9: 'If we confess our sins, he is faithful and just to forgive us our sins, and to cleanse us from all unrighteousness.'"

Many years have passed since that day, but that was my first introduction to those particular verses of Scripture, and I find them as helpful now as they were then! Something else that I'll never forget were the words this lady said to me, "WE'RE BEHIND YOU, MARGE!" Why, she really *cared!* It made a real difference to her. She may not have *completely* understood my problem, but she didn't condemn me.

NO ONE BEHIND YOU! My young friend was still talking . . . then I began to share with her my own experience. As I talked, I saw cold, steely eyes fill to the brim with tears, and a young, troubled face absolutely crumble before my very eyes. I was so thrilled to share with her the promise of God to those who are living on the edge of darkness. It was so wonderful to talk to her about King David, who out of a broken and contrite heart cried out, "Create in me a clean heart, O God; and renew a right spirit within me" (Psalm 51:10).

### We're Praying!

One day the youth director of our church came and asked me to write a letter to the young people who were away at college or in the service of our country. He wanted to let them know that we back home in their church loved and prayed for them always. As I wrote this letter, my thoughts went back to my own youth, and more recently to the young lady that I've told you about. I want to share this letter with you, because I received an answer to it that I think might be the answer some of you would send.

This is the letter that I wrote, which was mimeographed and sent out to all our college students and those young men in the service.

### HELLO, THERE!

As I sat here, thinking of you, I was wondering what on earth you are doing at this very moment. Are you, by any chance, sitting there thinking of home? of family? of friends? Do you ever get homesick for the uncomplicated life you led back here? Do you find yourself caught up in the complexities of pressures on every side? Are you like the college student who told me: "At home there in West Texas everything was either black or white—here it's gray! I'm afraid I'm going to like gray —I'm beginning not to mind it much!"

In this wonderful, yet terrifying, world in which we live today, you young people have a great challenge— greater than ever before in history. We adults cannot really tell you how and what to do, for we have made such horrible mistakes ourselves—and to put it honestly, we do not know!

Ah! But *you*, our beloved *young* person, let me tell you something to which we can *all* hold! Truth is the greatest source of personal power; love is the expression of that power in our lives. Oh, you've heard that before? I know you've heard it tritely said *so* many times—and hypocritically expressed by those pseudo-loving adults in our society today—ah! but it is *so true*—and the very source of all of this is our Lord Jesus Christ! I think I can almost tell what you're thinking right now—It's not that simple! Aren't you remembering that last conversation with friend or acquaintance when you were shaken inside spiritually— when everything you'd always taken for granted about our Lord was challenged and broken? Or has the thought crossed your mind—I just can't cope with that now. I'll think about it later!

Let me open my heart to you. And this heart represents the heart of your church—for we love you, we pray for you so often, and we're concerned about *you!* We are aware of *some* of the pressures of your life—not all, that's true, but some of them—and we know that in times like these, you need an anchor! No matter what "they" say—God never changes! Right is right—wrong is wrong—and Jesus Christ is the answer to the world—and our own personal life! Doesn't it make you feel more secure to know that back home there is a group of people who believe this implicitly—a church that preaches from God's Bible the unsearchable riches of his love—an "anchor" of prayer that God will be very near and dear to you? Well, this is something you can *count* on! When things get tough and you feel pushed and pressured on every side—when you're wondering who you *really* are, how you can make it, where you're going and why, what it's all about—when you're tempted physically, mentally, emotionally, and spiritually—then please think of us loving you and praying for you! And we *care!* And *Christ* cares!

So right now, whatever you're doing, visualize us holding your hand and saying, "You're the greatest. We're counting on you to be your *best* self for Jesus Christ! Not somebody else's best self—but *yours!*"

We love you sincerely,

MARGE CALDWELL

I received many letters in response. One filled me with deep concern, for it told of the pressures under which the high-school students of my hometown lived. Let me share some quotations from that unsigned letter:

[Our] parents are, generally speaking, very conscientious. They do their best to bring their children up right. So they take them to church . . .

We were, basically, good Christian young people . . .

[But] when I really needed some help in how to live what we were taught—I didn't know where to turn . . . I never really absorbed how to live as a Christian in the "wild" atmosphere of high school.

You wouldn't believe some of the activities Junior and Senior high-school students indulge in these days! . . . with that kind of atmosphere . . . how can one keep from straying from God? I haven't talked to God in at least three years, and I'm only a freshman in college . . .

I'm bitter because I have recently seen the error of my ways . . .

I felt that I needed to answer this student. So, in my next church letter, I said, among other things:

I've been on many high-school and college campuses . . . the conditions that you speak of exist on *every* one! It's a dilemma of our times, and my heart goes out to the high-school student who has any moral integrity or Christian conviction—for I *know* what the pressures are! As I go to these campuses, I have constant personal conferences and I know you're right—drinking, smoking, making out, cheating, stealing are just a popular as eating, and about as common! But you left out perversion and dope—and I've found *that,* too!

As to the pressure put on you young people to attend the church services, I know how you feel there, too! I *hated* Sunday School and Training Union while in high school, and even during college—and my mother *made* me go—and checked to see if I was in my class, and I was grounded *most* for lack of interest in the church! I used to wonder *why* all of this? Then I became a parent and found myself faced with exactly the same problem my mother had! Young people need to be challenged above all else—and thank God for their enthusiasm and optimism—but this all needs to be *challenged!* We need the sharpest, most intelligent, deeply spiritual teachers and leaders in our churches to teach and lead Intermediates and Young People—and we don't always have them!

But God has to use those who will *let* him use them—and sometimes the very best Christian cannot always teach a young person so that he can grasp the great truth involved. Then on the other hand, I found that I'd be enthralled with a person's ability to teach and be sick inside with disillusionment when I'd see the failure in their lives! So the combination of good teacher and committed Christian is of supreme value—yet sometimes rare! Please pray for our teachers and leaders in this particular area that they will sense the deep need of their students and let God lead them to help.

But back to our parents. They are frustrated, too—hoping that keeping that young person in church will somehow tie him to the Lord with an unbreakable rope—to hold him close to God in spite of himself. Hence, the pressure on attendance! But *you* know that attendance without love "profiteth nothing"—and coupled with the natural teen-age rebellion—will send you far away from Christ! So there is still a dilemma here!

As I read your letter, I yearned to talk to you! Yes, I know that many of our "faithful" young people are sitting in church, looking innocent and naïve, when they are spiritual schizophrenics—living one life in church and quite another outside! There are many adults doing the same! But each pays his own price for this in guilty conscience and loss of fellowship with Christ! Where is the virile, excited, thrilled, challenged Christian young person? Oh, how we pray that one of *you* will decide to be *that person!* Any town could be changed—your campus could—with just a few who decided that they'd try!

I know what you're thinking! Not *me!* I hardly *know* God any more. You said you hadn't talked to him in three years! And you weren't sure you were even saved as a youngster . . . I believe you *were!* And if you *were*—then you still *are!* You haven't lost your salvation—you have lost fellowship with Christ—and the *joy* that comes with that fellowship. How do I know? Because you wrote that letter and all through it I detected a tiny desire to find your way back to God! I was so excited I nearly burst when I read a line of your letter—and remembered a young lady at Rice University years ago who said these same words to a great adult Christian. This young lady was Marge—yes, yours truly, and I was told by this wise Christian that like David of old I could pray, "Create in me a clean heart, O God; and renew a right spirit within me" (Psalm 51:10). David had been far, far away from God, too—and he thought coming back was almost an impossibility also!

Thank you, dear writer, for a sweet, *not* bitter, letter—and may our other readers who identify with any part of this letter, ask God to lead them back, too. He can, and he will!

Sincerely, in Christ<br>MARGE CALDWELL

Many letters came from those in the service, and I'd like to share with you these excerpts from one:

I know that our young people at home do have a lot ahead of them . . . and, like some of them, I, too, have lost fellowship with Christ. Marge, I am like that young man that has been far, far away from God. . . . I also thought that coming back was almost impossible. In God's name, I pray, too, "Create in me a clean heart, O God!" . . .

I have seen my friends die beside me and have seen much blood spilled on this battlefield. I also wonder, Why wasn't it me. . . . not him? Why is it so important that *I* live and my buddy die? Of this I am not sure! However, I think there's a reason for my being left. . . . but I haven't gotten home yet either!

If it's God's will that my life be taken, like many have, then I pray that I can regain fellowship with him for the time I have left here!

I hope that you can understand what I have tried to say. I'm not very good at putting my thoughts on paper. Please pray for me as I fight, not only here in Vietnam, but fight my way back to God.

WE'RE BEHIND YOU! We're behind you young people with our prayers. We know we, as adults, have left you a hate-filled and turbulent world. We're certainly not proud of the conditions that exist all over the earth today. We did not have, as young people, some of the problems and perplexities that you're having to cope with today. We have no right to say to you, "When *I* was a girl . . .!" because conditions today are not like they were when we were young. But *people* are always the same! We had the same feelings of heartache, trouble, tragedy, joy, and thrills that you have today. The conditions behind these emotions are different, but the *emotions* are not! We suffer, and cry, and laugh, and love, and hate, just as we always have down through the ages.

Always remember, no matter how black it looks to you at the time, there are those who love you and belive in you—and, yes, *ARE BEHIND YOU!*

The most important thing for you to remember, however, is that no matter what "they" say—God is *not* dead! Listen! They've been saying that for ages. In the book of Psalms, we find, "The fool hath said in his heart, There is no God" (53:1). God is very much alive . . . he made you . . . he loves you . . . and he wants you to be the very best person you can possibly be!

# 6

## WHAT THEN—A.D. 2000?

Let's see! How old will you be in A.D. 2000? Maybe you'll be forty-five years old. Or fifty. Or even fifty-five. What a horrible thought! Why, that's old enough to *die* . . . looking at it from your point of view! Well, if you haven't "got it made" by then, it's just too late. Is that what you're thinking? In some ways, this might be true . . . but it's really never too late to become what you've always wanted to be.

You had wanted to accomplish so many things. You intended to travel and see the world . . . if we hadn't blown it up before you could afford to go! You had become interested in interior decorating . . . or was it music . . . or modeling . . . or journalism? You knew it would take a lot of study, and lots of time, and you were impatient! You loved to think of the future and dream. The future had held so many exciting opportunities for you. But somewhere along the way things began to get out of hand. Now the future is no longer the future . . . but the present! What became of all those exciting, ambitious dreams? Where did they vanish? What became of all those bright, young hopes? How many of your years have already passed . . . how many remain?

## Let's Dream!

Are you today secretary to the president of a large oil company? You have tremendous responsibilities and you're considered one of the most valued employees they have. You've been with this company a long time and have helped your husband financially put two sons through college. Your colleagues respect you, and you and your husband have many friends. However, deep down inside there's a void that comes up and haunts you from time to time. Was this what you had in mind for your future?

You will hardly admit it to yourself, but you feel a keen disappointment in your marriage. Somewhere along the years the romance seemed to disappear. One day you woke up and the line of communication between you and that boy you were so in love with seemed to have gone. It hurt so much, you just ignored it, and now the chasm between you is as wide as Grand Canyon! Where is that person . . . that marriage . . . that you dreamed of?

Oh, but *that's* not your case? Let's take another look. You have become famous! You're not only famous but very wealthy. You set a course for the future and, with dogged determination, you stuck to it. You went on to graduate school after college, and secured a wonderful position with a famous magazine. With pure hard work and lots of ambition, you finally reached your goal . . . you are now the editor of that magazine! Wherever you go, people know you. You've been a guest on many television shows and you've written some articles that have attracted national attention. You are sought after as an after-dinner speaker. At night, when you're alone, you often catch yourself thinking of the young man you parted with many years ago.

What a wild teen-ager you were! How you were attracted to that college freshman when you met him your senior year in high school! The months passed and you fell madly in love with him. He seemed to care for you, too, but you weren't sure of him. Then the night when your affair with him began . . . and the next months of torture and misery as you lived in horror that people would find out! You still cringe when you remember his face when you told him you were pregnant. Your trip to a large city a great distance away . . . the horror of those months . . . the baby you never saw . . . then taking up the threads of your life . . . and college! And now, you're wondering where that young dream became distorted. But as you reminisce about that young girl that you were, you remember your dream! What you had desperately wanted was a stable marriage with happy, laughing children, and a home full of love.

Let's take another look. Here you sit, bored and unhappy, with all that it takes for the average person to find satisfaction in life. You have a loving husband who has provided for you and the children in a wonderful way. He's not the most exciting person in the world, but he's dependable and kind. You have three wonderful children, two girls and a boy. According to most people's standards, you should be extremely happy and satisfied. But you're not. You're utterly miserable! You have been a spoiled and selfish person all your life . . . you've always known it! And now you're reaping the results of that selfish life.

You really didn't mean to become an alcoholic. You drank as a young person and were proud of the fact that you "could take it or leave it alone." You don't know exactly when it happened, but, somewhere along the way, you began to drink a little more heavily. Then you really became bored and sought release in steady drinking. How repulsed you've always been at the sight of a drunk woman! How sick you've been the next day, time after time, when you've seen the miserable look on your husband's face. And your children! Oh, you could hardly stand to face them and their hurt and disillusionment! Where did it start? What has happened to you? Where is the person you meant to be?

Or could this be you: You've struggled and worked with a wonderful husband to provide for those two children that God gave you. They're both teen-agers now, and one is getting ready to go off to college next year. Your home has always been like Macy's Department Store at Christmas—*you* know, crowded!—with all the young friends of your children. They have come and gone like the hotcakes that you've cooked for hours on end on Saturday mornings. Your home isn't elegant or expensively furnished, but it has always rung with laughter and fun. You and your husband are deeply in love and both of you love and serve God, along with your children. You have taught them to have the courage of their convictions, and to recognize the power that God can and will implant in their lives. You're proud of these two children! Oh, you know they've not always done things exactly right, but as you've exchanged confidences with them in the wee hours of the morning, you've thanked God for their courage. And you remember how it was when you were a teen-ager.

### What Is Yet to Be!

But let's come back to the present. You haven't even lived those years yet and all of this was just in our imagination. Aren't you glad you haven't, and that you have a chance to be the person that you really want to become? So I'll tell you what to do: look around you! Look at the friends you run with . . . the books you read . . .

the movies you see . . . the language you use . . .
whether you cheat or not! Take a good, long look at
these things. Better still remember that we were going
to take a mirror and take an honest look at ourselves?
Take up that mirror and look! Makes you sick? Then
take God's hand while you look, and, with his help,
try to be the best YOU that could possibly be!

### Reality . . . the Future!

One day I sat down in an easy chair.
  Put my feet up and laid back my head—
Then the ambitions and dreams—yes—I have my share—
  Began to crowd and rush through my head!

What do I want out of life? What's the end? What's my
    goal?
  These questions I thought through and through.
I'm young, ambitious, excited and thrilled—
  Isn't my story yet to come true?

A nurse? A model? Much money or fame?
  Oh, yes! Happiness then I would find!
That's it! I thought. That's what I'll attain!
  Why didn't that settle my mind?

My thoughts ran on and my heart told me this,
  "You're only a girl with so much to learn."
My heart said again, "Fame leaves but a kiss,
  Nothing else remains but the burn."

"And money," I said, "Is it not great?
  Such power, such freedom it gives?"
My heart said again, "Not money, my child,
  Only God shows a girl how to live!"

Not money or fame—they do not impart
  The security that you must possess,

It's something deep down in a young girl's heart,
   And she just can't settle for less!

So I'll strive for that love that God gives his child,
   And keep my eyes on the road—
And as I seek to help another in trial,
   I'll find that God has lightened *my* load!

MARGE CALDWELL